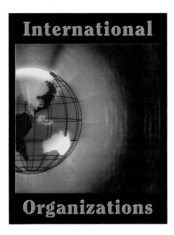

International Organizations

European Union

Petra Press

WORLD ALMANAC® LIBRARY

Please visit our web site at: www.worldalmaclibrary.com
For a free color catalog describing World Almanac® Library's list
of high-quality books and multimedia programs, call 1-800-848-2928 (USA)
or 1-800-387-3178 (Canada). World Almanac® Library's fax: (414) 332-3567.

Library of Congress Cataloging-in-Publication Data

Press, Petra.
    European Union / by Petra Press.
      p. cm. — (International organizations)
    Summary: Describes the background, formation, activities, advantages, and
disadvantages of the organization to which 15 European nations now belong.
    Includes bibliographical references and index.
    ISBN 0-8368-5518-3 (lib. bdg.)
    ISBN 0-8368-5527-2 (softcover)
    1. European Union—Juvenile literature. [1. European Union.] I. Title.
II. International organizations (Milwaukee, Wis.)
JN30.P745   2003
341.242'2—dc21   2003047940

First published in 2004 by
World Almanac® Library
330 West Olive Street, Suite 100
Milwaukee, WI 53212 USA

Developed by Books Two, Inc.
Editor: Jean B. Black
Design and Maps: Krueger Graphics, Inc.: Karla J. Krueger and Victoria L. Buck
Indexer: Chandelle Black
World Almanac® Library editor: JoAnn Early Macken
World Almanac® Library art direction: Tammy Gruenewald

Photo Credits: All photos courtesy Audiovisual Library European Commission, except the follow-
ing: © AFP/CORBIS: 38; Agricultural Research Service/Scott Bauer: 15; © Bettmann/CORBIS: 23;
© CICR/HEGER, Boris: 31; © Jose Fuste Raga/CORBIS: 34; National Archives: 5; Reuters/Lee Jae
Won: 35; Reuters/MARIO LAPORTA: 30

Printed in the United States of America

1 2 3 4 5 6 7 8 9 07 06 05 04 03

TABLE OF CONTENTS

Words that appear in the glossary are printed in
boldface type the first time they occur in the text.

Chapter One

Citizens of Europe

Imagine that people in the United States were allowed to live, work, and travel only within the state in which they were born. A family in Ohio would need special written permission to look for work in Indiana. They would need special passports to vacation at Disneyland.

People would think of themselves first and foremost as Ohioans or Californians or New Yorkers, not Americans. Schools in one state might be much better than in another. Workers would have more rights in some states. Living in the United States would be like living in fifty different countries.

The discussions that eventually led to the formation of the European Union (EU) began soon after World War II. It wasn't until the members passed a special agreement called the Maastricht Treaty in 1993 that most people living in the forty-three countries that make up Europe began to think of themselves as "Europeans." Instead, they thought of themselves as citizens of the country they were born in, such as Italy, Sweden, or Spain. Most still do. The Maastricht Treaty, however, made everyone living in an EU member country citizens of Europe as well as their own country.

This is a tremendously important concept because the treaty allows people to move freely from one country to another. It allows them to look for work anywhere they want within the EU. They can vote in any member country, even if they are not citizens of that country.

Young people in Europe today have a chance to live very different lives than their grandparents did because of changes made by the European Union.

Even more important, many people now think of issues in terms of how they affect all of Europe, not just the country they live in. A family in Ireland, for example, may now be more concerned about making schools better, protecting the environment, and raising workplace standards for everyone throughout Europe. They may now care about women's rights in Estonia and the flow of Turkish migrants into Germany. Their concern has increased because they are citizens of a unified Europe.

The end of World War II in 1945 left much of Europe, such as this village in Germany, destroyed. Europeans became determined not to allow war between their countries again.

"Let Europe Arise!"

In the fall of 1946, much of Europe was rubble and devastation. Fifty million people died in the fighting that took place between 1939 and 1945. Six million Jews died in **Nazi** concentration camps, along with several million people from other ethnic groups. Another forty million people were homeless. The war was over, but the despair was overwhelming. Winston Churchill, prime minister of England, gave a speech that challenged despairing Europeans to see themselves in a whole new way:

"I wish to speak to you today about the tragedy of Europe. If Europe were once united in the sharing of its common inheritance, there would be no limit to the happiness, to the prosperity and the glory . . . its . . . people would enjoy. Yet it is from Europe that have sprung that series of frightful **nationalistic** quarrels [that] wreck the peace and mar the prospects of all mankind. . . .

The Rise of Nationalism

The idea of a unified Europe had actually been around for thousands of years. Political, military, and even religious leaders gobbled up each other's kingdoms and carved up the continent to create vast empires. Then they made the people they conquered conform to their own cultures. The Roman, Byzantine, Holy Roman, and Hapsburg empires were just a few of the attempts to "unify" Europe. The idea of "nations" spread in the mid-nineteenth century when conquered peoples began to resent being dominated by a foreign culture. Each culture wanted to form a separate, independent nation. Eventually, countries such as Germany, Austria, Italy, and France won their independence.

Some of these new nations took nationalism too far. They began to squabble with each other over borders. They formed armies. By the early twentieth century, more violent conflicts broke out. Conflicts exploded into the two bloodiest wars of all time. More than twenty-one million people died in World War I. More than fifty million died in World War II.

"Over wide areas a vast quivering mass of tormented, hungry, care-worn and bewildered human beings gape at the ruins of their cities and their homes, and scan the dark horizons for the approach of some new peril, tyranny or terror. . . . Yet all the while there is a remedy which . . . would in a few years make all Europe, or the greater part of it . . . free and . . . happy. . . . What is this sovereign remedy? It is to re-create the European Family, or as much of it as we can, and to provide it with a structure under which it can dwell in peace, in safety and in freedom. We must build a kind of United States of Europe . . . and we must champion [its] right to live and shine. Therefore I say to you: let Europe arise!"

Stirred by Churchill's vision of a unified Europe, many people agreed that nationalism was the cause of wars and other European problems. People wanted peace and unity. But their most overwhelming concern was rebuilding their war-torn cities and ravaged farms. Bombed-out factories needed to be rebuilt to provide jobs. People needed money to buy food, clothing, and building materials. Any plan to unify Europe had to start by rebuilding, literally from the ground up.

A First Step: Coal and Steel

Within a short time after the end of World War II, it became clear that France and West Germany were going to argue continually about the right to the Ruhr Valley, which is the center of Europe's coal and steel industries. Two Frenchmen came up with an amazing plan they thought would help prevent future wars. At the same time, it would help rebuild Europe. A brilliant French statesman named Jean Monnet had spent years working with the old League of Nations, the predecessor of the United Nations. Monnet and a French foreign minister named Robert Schuman came up with the idea of European nations joining together to control coal and steel production. Their plan became known as the Schuman Plan.

Monnet and Schuman's reasoning was simple. Coal and steel were the raw materials of war. They were used to make guns, tanks, and ammunition. The two men created a plan to keep track of how much

Jean Monnet and Robert Schuman knew that the redevelopment of Europe after World War II would depend on coal and steel, such as is used in this Audi plant in Hungary.

Jean Monnet (1888-1979)

Jean Monnet was a successful businessman who hoped that the League of Nations, which was formed after World War I, would lead to peace around the world. He soon accepted that because of the way the League was structured, peace and harmony were not going to happen. The League settled some smaller international disputes and provided humanitarian aid to countries in need, but many member countries, such as Germany and Japan, refused to abide by the League's decisions in larger disputes.

Instead, Monnet concentrated on business dealings throughout Europe in the 1930s. In 1940, the American, French, and British governments asked him to serve as an economic military advisor. He came up with a desperate and brilliant plan that could have changed the entire course of World War II. The French army was unable to stop Nazi troops. To save them, Monnet proposed that France and Great Britain unite to form an Anglo-French Union. The new nation would pool its troops and resources. He presented the plan to British Prime Minister Winston Churchill and the leader of the Free French, Charles de Gaulle. The leaders actually considered accepting it, but by then, it was too late. France had already surrendered to Nazi Germany.

After World War II ended, Monnet saw that to remain free from future wars, European countries had to work together in all ways possible. The European Union was the eventual result of his ideas. In the late 1940s and early 1950s, Monnet was awarded many honors for his efforts to promote peaceful and strong economic ties between nations. The honors include the Presidential Medal of Freedom, the highest civilian medal awarded by the United States. Monnet is seen in the photo above about to turn the handle to release the first steel produced by the European Coal and Steel Community in 1953.

coal and steel each country produced. It would also keep track of how the coal and steel were used. Such an agreement would make it very hard for one member country to stockpile weapons for war against another. It would also make sure that all the coal and steel produced would be used to rebuild factories, homes, railroads, and schools.

Five other countries accepted the French proposal: Belgium, West Germany, Italy, Luxembourg, and the Netherlands. On April 18, 1951, these countries—which came to be known as "The Six"—formed the European Coal and Steel Community (ECSC). Within five years, these same countries made great strides in rebuilding their factories and cities.

The ECSC proved to be a very important first step. Farms produced more and better food. Governments provided better health care, more plentiful housing, and easier access to higher education. Trains and other mass transportation made cheap travel possible. Many people started earning enough to buy luxuries, such as television sets and cars.

Strength in Unity

By the mid-1950s, the rebuilding of Western Europe had made tremendous prog-ress. Much of it was the result

In 1953, a train carrying flags and coal crossed the border between France and Luxembourg to celebrate the first ore produced by the ECSC.

Vespas, Volkswagens, and Bic Pens

Some very creative and successful business ventures rose out of the rubble of World War II using the coal and steel regulated by the ESCS. Enrico Piaggio's Italian aircraft factory had been almost completely destroyed by bombs. He got his chief engineer to design a new form of cheap transportation that could be produced in what was left of the factory. Piaggio named the zippy little motor scooters Vespas ("wasps"). He sold millions of these little buzzing machines all over Europe.

In 1937, Adolf Hitler had commissioned Ferdinand Porsche to design a low-priced *Volkswagen*, meaning "people's car." Production was interrupted by the war, and the factory was destroyed. When West Germany started to rebuild after the war, German businessmen got together and rebuilt the industry. A decade later, they were selling millions of Volkswagens all over the world.

A French manufacturer named Marcel Bich had to rebuild his bombed-out fountain pen factory. He ran into a Hungarian inventor with a patent for a revolutionary new ballpoint pen. Bich bought the patent and was soon manufacturing "Bic" pens. They quickly changed the writing habits of people the world over.

All of these products remain popular throughout Europe, especially the scooters (above), which make getting around easier in Europe's old inner cities.

of the U.S. Marshall Plan. In this plan, devised by U.S. Secretary of State George C. Marshall in 1947, the United States provided huge amounts of money and building materials to get homes rebuilt and factories restarted. Rebuilding projects created jobs and new industries. People had money to buy manufactured goods. Economies prospered again.

Once they started producing and trading goods again, Europeans realized that progress could be a lot faster. Every European country charged its own import and export **tariffs**, or taxes. Every kind of manufactured good or food product had tariffs that were supposed to keep foreign goods out of the country. However, these tariffs often hurt each nation's own merchants, manufacturers, and farmers because they could not stay

Representatives of The Six—France, Belgium, West Germany, Italy, Luxembourg, and the Netherlands—established the European Economic Community and EURATOM by signing the first Treaty of Rome on March 25, 1957.

in business if they couldn't sell their goods in other European countries.

In 1955, The Six of the ECSC met in Rome to talk about expanding their agreements to eliminate these trading hassles. In 1957, a treaty went into effect that created the European Economic Community (EEC), which was soon called simply the Common Market. The EEC removed many trading barriers between member countries. The goal of the EEC was to create one single European market that would ensure the free movement of goods and services between member nations.

Another concern of many Europeans in the 1950s was atomic (nuclear) energy. They knew about the terrible death and destruction atomic bombs had brought to Japan. They were horrified about the possibilities of the development of atomic weapons. At the same time, they saw the positive applications the atom could have as a new, cheap source of energy. In their 1955 meeting in Rome, the Six also created the European Atomic Energy Community (EURATOM). Its primary purpose was to oversee the building of nuclear power plants to create electricity.

Six Plus Six and Beyond

By the late 1960s, the ECSC, the Common Market, and EURATOM officially merged into one organization that became known as the European Community, or EC. In 1973, Denmark, Ireland, and the United Kingdom joined the first six nations in the EC. Greece joined in 1981. Spain and Portugal joined in 1986.

Not all European countries became members. Norway's citizens voted 52 to 48 percent not to join, mainly because Norway had been an independent country for less than a century and was reluctant to give up any power. Also, the fact that Norway owns much of the oil found under the North Sea means that the country doesn't need the economic help that EU membership might bring.

In 1992, in a meeting at Maastricht, Netherlands, the role of the European Community was expanded. The members decided that

Berlaymont in Brussels, Belgium, was built in 1966 as the headquarters of the Common Market. The whole operation of the European Union has since expanded into many buildings throughout Europe.

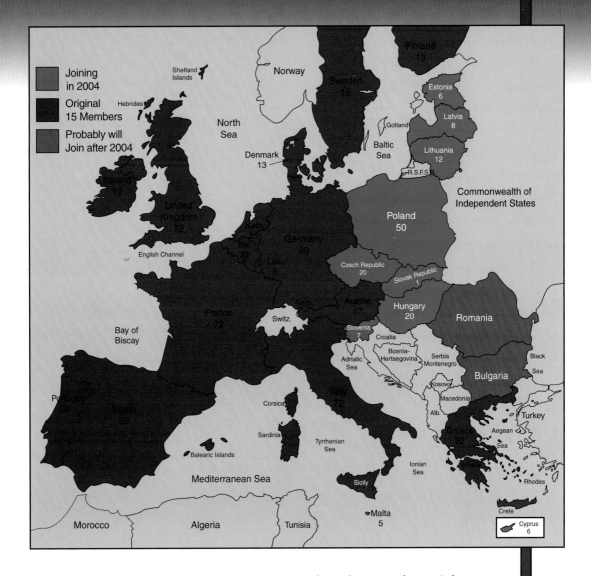

from then on, they would meet to vote on political issues that might affect them, as well as economic matters. Member countries would set policies on issues such as **human rights** and environmental protection. These policies would govern all the people living in member countries. European citizens would now have a strong voice in shaping international politics as well. While the member countries were at it, they decided that the Maastricht Treaty would gave this new form of the combined organizations (ECSC, EC, and EURATOM) a new name. It became the European Union, or EU. The Maastricht Treaty officially went into effect in 1993. The EU expanded again in 1995 when three new members were added: Austria, Finland, and Sweden.

Most member countries also drafted an agreement to develop a single form of currency, or money. They called this new currency the euro. The euro became the official currency of most of Europe on January 1, 2002.

In December 2000, the fifteen member countries wrote the Treaty of Nice, which established the basis for enlarging the EU to twenty-seven members. In 2004, ten new members will bring the total to twenty-five. Those members are Poland, Hungary, the Czech Republic, Slovakia, Slovenia, Estonia, Lithuania, Latvia, Malta, and Cyprus. Romania and Bulgaria are expected to be ready for membership in 2007.

Introduction to the Maastricht Treaty

By this Treaty, the HIGH CONTRACTING PARTIES establish among themselves a EUROPEAN UNION, hereinafter called "the Union."

DETERMINED to lay the foundations of an ever closer union among the peoples of Europe,

RESOLVED to ensure the economic and social progress of their countries by common action to eliminate the barriers which divide Europe,

AFFIRMING as the essential objective of their efforts the constant improvements of the living and working conditions of their peoples,

RECOGNIZING that the removal of existing obstacles calls for concerted action in order to guarantee steady expansion, balanced trade and fair competition,

ANXIOUS to strengthen the unity of their economies and to ensure their harmonious development by reducing the differences existing between the various regions and the backwardness of the less-favored regions,

DESIRING to contribute, by means of a common commercial policy, to the progressive abolition of restrictions on international trade,

INTENDING to confirm the solidarity which binds Europe and the overseas countries and desiring to ensure the development of their prosperity, in accordance with the principles of the Charter of the United Nations,

RESOLVED by thus pooling their resources to preserve and strengthen peace and liberty, and calling upon the other peoples of Europe who share their ideal to join in their efforts,

DETERMINED to promote the development of the highest possible level of knowledge for their peoples through a wide access to education and through its continuous updating,

HAVE DECIDED to create a EUROPEAN COMMUNITY.

The EU at Work

In the mid-1980s, news-papers carried a small story of cattle dying in Great Britain of a fatal disease that eats away at the muscles and brain. It was identified as bovine spongiform encephalopathy, or BSE. In West Germany, Ute Menna and her husband Klaus vaguely remembered reading about it in the weekly magazine *Der Spiegel*. The epidemic was aggravating to British farmers, of course. But it wasn't really anything

With the spread of Creutzfeldt-Jakob (or "mad cow") disease in the 1990s, many cattle and sheep had to be destroyed in European Union countries. It will take years for European farmers to rebuild their herds and flocks.

that concerned this German couple who ran a shop selling pewter mugs in Frankfurt. It certainly didn't stop them from eating beef. Their eight-year-old daughter, Annemarie, loved hamburgers. She often stopped in at the nearby McDonald's on her way home from school. Klaus ordered steak every time they went out to eat, and Ute's entertaining specialty was pot roast with dumplings.

In March of 1996,the Mennas were shocked by a newscast about a new, horrible epidemic in Great Britain. Dozens of people had died slow, painful deaths. A terrible infection had eaten away at their brains and muscles. Scientists called the condition in humans Creutzfeldt-Jakob disease after the scientists who described it. They said that it might be linked to eating beef from cows infected with BSE.

PRIMARY STRUCTURE OF THE

EUROPEAN COMMISSION

* Proposes new laws and policies
* Negotiates international treaty agreements
* One Commissioner is appointed by each member country
* Treaty of Nice increases number of Commissioners from fifteen to twenty-five
* Treaty of Nice sets maximum seats at twenty-seven
* Headquarters is the Secretariat in Brussels

PRESIDENT

* President of the Commission most important figure in EU
* Decides the Commission's priority issues
* Takes part in meetings of the European Council
* Takes part in the major debates of the European Parliament
* Takes part in political negotiations with other government leaders
* Is appointed by the governments of the member states for five-year term
* Treaty of Nice expanded president's powers: he or she can now assign policy issues to certain commissioners or ask them to resign

COURT OF JUSTICE

* Court assures that the EU's laws and treaties are enforced
* One judge is appointed per member state
* Treaty of Nice increases number of justices from fifteen to twenty-five
* Court's responsibilities are not changed by the Treaty of Nice
* Located in Luxembourg (See photo on page 22.)

Ute and Klaus panicked. People all over Europe panicked. Almost every country imported at least some of its beef from Great Britain. Even people who didn't eat imported beef were terrified that the disease had spread to cattle in other countries. That's how the serious cattle killer hoof-and-mouth disease spread. And what if the human version itself was contagious? Headlines all over the world screamed "mad cow disease!" There was no cure.

EUROPEAN UNION

COUNCIL OF MINISTERS

* Votes on laws and policies
  proposed by European Commission
  and European Parliament
* Votes on budget matters
* Made up of Ministers who are
  also cabinet members in the
  governments of their home
  countries
* Treaty of Nice increases membership from 87 to 171 and lowers the
  percentage of votes needed to
  pass certain laws
* Headquarters is in Brussels

EUROPEAN PARLIAMENT

* Debates laws and policies but cannot vote on them
* Representatives elected directly by citizens in member countries every five years
* Treaty of Nice increases number of members from 626 to 732
* Treaty of Nice increases its power: it can also now propose some laws and policies
* Meets in Strasbourg, Brussels, and Luxembourg (See photos on pages 20 and 21.)

Like many Europeans, Ute and Klaus immediately stopped buying beef. They forbade Annemarie to visit McDonald's. News reports of the epidemic got worse. By 2000, over eighty people had died of mad cow disease. Britain's $6.5 billion-a-year beef industry was on the point of collapse. Beef prices everywhere else were down 50 percent and more. Thousands of cattle were destroyed simply because they might have been in contact with infected animals.

Ute's fears grew, especially for her daughter. Although her family stopped eating beef, Ute began to suspect that other foods could also be harmful. She avoided buying any foods with chemical **additives**. Ute also began to suspect that **hormones** had been secretly added to the milk and cheese. Even their vegetables might have been fertilized with something poisonous. The Mennas were not the only ones scared and concerned. People all over Europe demanded that the EU take steps to protect them.

The EU Reacts

The EU is not the government of a single nation made up of individual states the way the United States is comprised of fifty states. The individual governments of the member nations of the EU still make and enforce most of the laws that govern the people living in those countries. Many of these laws differ from country to country. Individual nations send representatives to the EU to debate and vote on issues that affect Europe as a whole. Some of these issues have to do with situations within European borders, such as trade and environmental protection. The EU also votes on policies regarding its political and economic interaction with other nations throughout the world.

The EU is similar in some ways to the government of the United States. Laws and policies do not change quickly. Even on important matters, the planning for new legislation is usually a slow, thoughtful, and deliberate process. There is also more than one legislative body involved in making decisions. Those bodies enact the EU's laws and policies. No single body could quickly react to the BSE crisis.

In 2000, EU President Romano Prodi directed the European Commission to consider the urgent matter of mad cow disease. However, the European Commission cannot vote to enact laws and policies. It can only propose laws for the other bodies of the EU to debate and vote on.

The Commission is made up of government representatives sent by each of the member countries. Each commissioner is an expert in a certain policy area, such as transportation, agriculture, environment, or health. Each is given a staff of several hundred people.

For example, the mad cow disease matter was given to the agricultural commissioners. They and their staffs researched every aspect of the issue. Their research included consulting doctors, veterinarians, scientists, and farmers and even interviewing the manufacturers of cattle feed. The commissioners investigated the causes of the deaths and calculated the impact of the problem. Their calculations included the terrible possibilities of epidemics and economic crashes. After analyzing their research, the commissioners drew up specific recommendations.

The commissioners decided that the most important consideration

At the height of the "mad cow" scare in 2000, all British beef was banned, and some nations refused to import beef from France. By 2001, Austria, Italy, and Finland had also had their first cases of BSE.

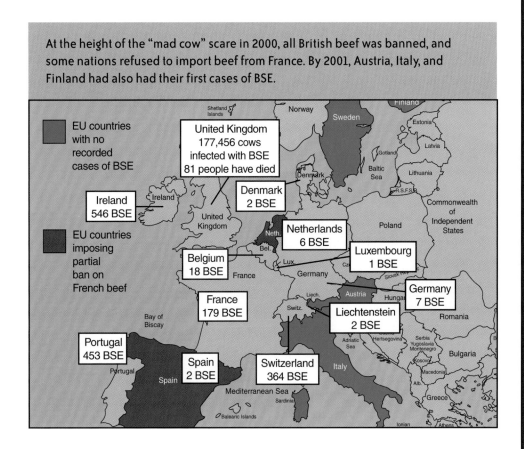

was to reassure the public, no matter what the cost, that the disease would not spread. They recommended that all cattle throughout the EU be tested at regular periods for signs of the disease. Infected cattle would be bought by the EU and destroyed. They calculated that it would cost about $7.7 million just to test the six million head of cattle on EU farms.

More Debate and Deliberation

The commissioners sent their recommendations to the European Parliament. Parliament is made up of 686 representatives who are directly elected for five-year terms by the people living in the EU.

Issues such as the mad cow disease epidemic are often hotly debated by the Parliament. In this case, many people wanted large numbers of

This chamber, called the Hemicycle, is the primary meeting place of the European Parliament in Strasbourg, France. It holds all 686 elected delegates.

cattle destroyed simply as a preventive health measure. Some thought the disease could spread to sheep, which they also wanted destroyed.

Farmers, on the other hand, were devastated by the effect of the scare on their profits. Their beef trade with countries all over the world had dropped drastically. This was especially true in Great Britain and France.

The members of the European Parliament meet in its Brussels building during most of each month for committee and political meetings.

Representatives who supported the farmers believed that people were overreacting. They thought that panic could ruin European economies. Some members objected because they didn't want the EU to spend so much money on the program.

In the end, the majority of members agreed with the Commission's recommendations. But Parliament is not allowed to actually vote on policies and laws either. They sent their recommendations and the Commission's to the Council of Ministers.

Finally, a Vote

The Council of Ministers actually votes on the laws recommended by the other two legislative bodies. The Council is made up of representatives who also serve as **cabinet ministers** in their home governments. The Council of Ministers quickly voted the recommendations into law.

People are still scared. In 2003, beef consumption in Europe was still less than 50 percent of what it had been ten years before. Europeans still disagree about the EU's policy on the matter, and the issue remains under study by the European Commission.

The European Court of Justice

What happens if a cattle farmer in France refuses to get his cattle tested? He may not have broken any French laws, but EU laws are the "law of the land." He can be prosecuted in front of the European Court of Justice, which is sometimes equated to the U.S. Supreme Court. He could be fined or even sent to prison.

The Court of Justice hears **appeals** on matters brought by the European Union's government. It also rules on matters concerning member countries, corporations, national governments, or private citizens. The Court's decisions are final and binding, which means they cannot be appealed. Member governments and all parties involved must abide by the decisions. Fifteen judges (the number will be twenty-five when the EU is expanded) serve the Court, each for a six-year term.

The European Court of Justice, which is made up of one judge from each member country, meets in Luxembourg.

Creating a People's Europe

Twelve-year old Heydar Burcu and his friends stand on top of crumbling stone walls in the hot sun. They stare for hours at the land they can see beyond a barbed-wire fence. The walls and barbed wire mark the barren United Nations-patrolled cease-fire zone. It divides the capital city of Nicosia, Cyprus, the way the Berlin Wall once divided the German city of Berlin, except that here it divides not just the capital city but the whole island country. The Cypriots call this dead zone the "Attila Line."

Cyprus lies in the northeastern corner of the Mediterranean Sea, about 40 miles (64 kilometers) south of Turkey and 60 miles (97 km) west of Syria. Heydar and the other Turkish Cypriots in the north are

Muslim. They are trapped behind the barbed wire in a desolate time-warp of a world. But many live close enough to the high-rise apartment buildings, billboards, and cars of the Greek half of the island to see what they are missing.

The Greek Cypriots are Orthodox Christians. Their government is open and democratic. Most people on the island are sick to death of the ethnic hatred and fighting and want to live in peace. But the ruler of the Turkish Cypriots, Rauf Denktash, is a

In 1964, Turkish Cypriots were forced from their homes by Greek Cypriot fighters. These women and children sought safety at a refugee camp near Nicosia. The island has been divided since then.

Turkish Tensions

Cyprus is scheduled to join the EU in 2004. This move could cause serious international complications. Turkey does not want to give up control of northern Cyprus and unite the Turkish and Greek Cypriots. It will take years of international **diplomacy** to get Turkey to agree to a united Cyprus. If it doesn't, fighting could break out between Greece and Turkey. Tensions between Turkey and the EU are already high because Turkey applied for 2004 EU membership but was rejected, mostly because of its human-rights record.

Meanwhile, an increasing number of Turks believe that many of the international policies of both the EU and the United States are growing more anti-Muslim. They don't want to have any political connections with Western nations. All this adds to already overheated tensions in the Middle East.

repressive dictator who forbids any attempts to unify the two parts of the island. He calls the Turkish part of the island the Turkish Republic of Northern Cyprus, but only Turkey recognizes it as a nation.

Today, however, it is not with anger or resentment that Heydar and his friends peer into that more affluent world. It is with hope. The EU has just voted the nation of Cyprus (which includes the Turkish Cypriots) to be one of the new members admitted to the Union in 2004, whether the north and south have been unified by that time or not. Membership will help his country tremendously. Heydar hopes that the barbed wire and crumbing walls of the dead zone will come down, bringing peace, and the EU will bring jobs and a healthy economy so that families like his can afford those things the billboards have been promising for so long.

The EU's "Celtic Tiger"

No one knows better than the Irish the dramatic changes that EU membership can bring. In 1973, the year it was admitted, the Republic of Ireland was struggling with high unemployment. Many families had left the country to find work elsewhere. By the late 1990s, however, Ireland had become one of the strongest economies in Europe. The EU had dedicated billions of dollars to help rebuild Ireland's roads and cities. The infusion of money helped build factories and provided start-up money for new industries. It also encouraged international computer companies such as Dell, Microsoft, and Apple to manufacture and distribute products there.

Mary McAleese, who became Ireland's second female president in 1997, remembers how people were scared of losing their Irish identity when Ireland joined the EU: "People thought we would be simply overwhelmed, our culture and language would be obliterated. Our sense of identity would be thrown into a stewpot, and we would just come out like some kind of amorphous clone. . . . What happened was that we were provided with this extraordinary showcase. It has sharpened our consciousness and our confidence in what it is to be Irish . . . we're proud of the things that we bring to the table precisely because they come out of our . . . historic and our present experience of being Irish."

A Better Standard of Living

The EU has changed the lives of many Europeans. For Carlos Fernández of Spain

An important part of improving Ireland's and other nations' economies is preparing for a growing number of tourists. These people are visiting a country inn.

and his wife, María Luisa, the EU has meant good-paying jobs. Carlos, a former factory worker, had been unemployed for over a year and still could not find work. His wife was working as a waitress. In 2000, a special EU employment program offered them both training in information technology. This enabled them to get jobs with Diesel Marine International right in their hometown of Algeciras. Their combined incomes are now paying for a new house in the suburbs.

The standard of living in Europe has doubled since the late 1950s. More people can afford to buy homes and cars. They buy high-tech electronics and other luxuries. They travel and enjoy fine restaurants. Even so, high unemployment has continued to be a major problem in many areas. More than thirteen million people in the EU are unemployed—over 8 percent of the workforce. Many people, especially immigrants, are still poor.

Since 1997, the EU has held a series of special European Work Councils throughout the EU. The Councils provide job counseling and high-tech vocational training. They also deal with international companies that open branch companies in Europe, and they make sure that European employees have adequate benefits, labor union representation,

These fishing-boat workers are preparing the day's catch for market. Catching, processing, and selling seafood are important to those European countries located on a sea. The EU is limiting the number of fishing boats to make sure that there will always be enough for everyone.

and health and safety standards. The Councils contributed to more than 60 percent of the jobs created in Europe between 1995 and 2000.

The EU has also set up agencies to protect consumers against unfair business practices. Companies are prosecuted if they manipulate their bookkeeping to make their stock prices go up. Companies are prevented from agreeing to keep prices on their goods unfairly high. Products must live up to their advertising.

The EU hopes to help citizens of Europe acquire skills that will keep them abreast of new technology, such as is being used by this European factory worker.

Unfortunately, not everyone gets help. The owners of many small, family-owned businesses want to keep their businesses, but the amount of paperwork they have to do is a burden. Also, regulations are hard on small-business owners. For example, EU laws force businesses of any size to pay all employees at a certain level, and no employee can be laid off without months of notice. The result is that many small-business owners are slow to take on new employees to expand their businesses.

Simplifying Life with the Euro

Imagine what it would be like if each of the fifty states of the United States had its own currency. A six-state drive to Disney World would

Both coins and bills in the single-currency system used by twelve nations since 2002 are called the euro. There is no longer a need to change money when crossing between two different countries that use the euro.

mean having to take along six different kinds of money just to pay for gas and food along the way. People would have to pay banking fees to exchange their money. Think of what a hassle it would be for farmers and retail companies. It would make doing business out of state so cumbersome and expensive that companies wouldn't bother shipping their goods or foods to other states at all. The government would have many problems collecting taxes.

That complicated situation is exactly what people living in Europe once experienced. That's why the EU invented the euro. Twelve of the fifteen member countries agreed to adopt a single, common currency. It went into effect in early 2002. The euro is now the only legal currency in those countries. There are no more lira, deutschmarks, or francs. Many people were reluctant to change, but they find the new system easier.

Saying "No" to the Euro

The people of the United Kingdom voted not to join the euro currency. The English pound sterling was, for centuries, the most important currency on Earth, and the British see no reason to give it up. Tony Blair, the prime minister as the twenty-first century started, hopes that he can make the British change their minds. Also choosing not to join the euro system were EU members Sweden and Denmark.

Health Care

Western Europe has some of the world's best doctors and most modern clinics and hospitals. People pay high taxes, but they also enjoy very low-cost public health-care systems. The European Union does not regulate or administer individual health-care systems. Instead, the EU concerns itself with issues that affect all member nations. For example, it sets policies for occupational health and safety standards, and it makes certain that medical training is equal for all nations.

The EU health ministers also develop action plans for dealing with emergency public health issues, such as the 2003 outbreak of the new highly communicable disease called SARS, for severe acute respiratory syndrome. While Asia was suffering a rapid growth in the number of SARS cases, only a few had reached European countries. However, the outbreak prompted the health ministers to plan a new Center for Disease Control, which might have the authority to establish health screenings at airports and other points of entry.

The EU's health concerns extend well beyond communicable diseases and well beyond its own boundaries. The EU and the World Health Organization (WHO) work together to address a wide range of other universal health issues, including the control of tobacco products; a global strategy on diet, physical activity and health; and global research into the impact of environment on health.

Illegal Immigrants

Another crisis EU lawmakers must deal with concerns illegal immigration. Immigrants want to escape the miseries of their homelands and find better lives. They come in small boats from Africa, the Balkans, the Middle East, Pakistan, and even China to reach the coasts of Spain, Italy, and Greece. Many drown in the process. Some try to enter Europe overland with falsified passports. Each year, thousands of Afghans, Kosovars, Kurds, and others try to sneak through the Channel Tunnel to get into Britain. Some huddle inside container trucks being smuggled in, and some even die there. Those who are caught are deported, or sent back, to their home countries.

In 2000, the Italian navy rescued a weather-tossed ship trying to smuggle more than twelve hundred Kurdish people from Turkey into Italy. Such illegal immigration is a major problem for the EU.

Most illegal immigrants are not caught. What should be done about them? Many people in the EU argue that these people are political **refugees** who should be given asylum, or safe refuge, because they are fleeing from repressive governments. Many EU citizens believe that immigrants should be welcomed into the workforce, pointing out that there are more than enough low-tech jobs available. These are jobs that most Europeans don't want, such as picking tomatoes in Spain.

A growing number of Europeans, however, insist that the immigrants are economic and not political refugees. Unemployed immigrants, they say, take job opportunities away from Europeans, and if the immigrants don't work, they increase crime and drug use and are an unfair burden on taxpayers. These Europeans want the EU to strengthen security at its borders. Some Europeans want immigrant families already living illegally in the EU arrested and sent back to their native lands.

Resentment of immigrants, both legal and illegal, is increasing in the EU. Lawmakers will have to decide exactly which people their "People's Europe" will include.

The EU and the World

In many places of the world today, people greatly resent the presence of U.S. peacekeeping troops and angrily protest that the troops be withdrawn. In Europe's war-torn Bosnia, however, many people are equally upset that U.S. troops are planning to leave in 2003. They are leaving because U.S. and other peacekeeping troops of NATO (the North Atlantic Treaty Organization) are being phased out in Bosnia. They are to be replaced by a new EU peacekeeping force. The European Union has never played a military role before. This inexperience has the people they will protect a little nervous.

Bosnia is one of the countries formed out of the former republic of Yugoslavia. In 1992, a bloody civil war broke out between two major ethnic groups, the Bosnian Serbs, who are Christian, and the segment of the population that is primarily Muslim. In February 1994, the two sides finally agreed to a cease-fire to be policed by troops of NATO. Ever since, it has been the job of the NATO force to protect civilians and arrest war criminals. U.S. troops have made up a majority of the NATO force.

In spite of the NATO presence, tensions between Bosnia's ethnic groups remain highly charged. Many refugees are still too afraid to return to their homes. A number of war criminals have been convicted, but not all have been tried or even apprehended. In other

A U.S. soldier in the NATO force in Bosnia in 2001 talks to a Red Cross volunteer.

words, Bosnia is still a frightening place to live and raise a family.

Bosnians want a reassuring peacekeeping presence. They feel safe with the presence of the U.S. troops. They're worried that the EU isn't ready to stand alone as a peacekeeping military force. Many Bosnians ask why their European neighbors didn't intervene in the early 1990s when the terrible fighting first broke out. They wonder why they should trust those other Europeans now.

Bosnia is not the only country paying attention to the EU's formation of a military force. European countries fought bitterly with each other for hundreds of years. Can they now overcome their rivalries to act with one military body? This will be the EU's first peacekeeping effort. The whole world will be watching.

> "As the people and countries of the Balkans move closer to Europe, it is only natural that Europe assume increasing leadership and responsibility. I welcome the European Union's commitment to play a leading role in the stabilization and development of the region. I similarly welcome the willingness of our allies to provide the bulk of the NATO task force.... The cooperation of the United States, NATO, and the EU ... is a model that we can build upon in the future."
> — *U.S. President George W. Bush, July 24, 2001*

Peace through Economic Stability

The EU was founded on the idea that peace depends on economic stability. The members found that the best way to achieve economic stability was through democratic partnership and free trade. That philosophy has also been very successful in the EU's relations with the rest of the world. The EU pushes for open markets and free trade all over the world, especially with developing nations. In the early 1990s, EU leaders decided their economic power gave them the responsibility to have a say in world politics as well as trade. The Maastricht Treaty created a part of the EU government to make foreign policies and agreements.

The EU became political because times had changed. Soviet control of Central and Eastern Europe collapsed in 1991. The collapse of the Soviet

The EU hopes to help the Eastern European countries that are in the process of joining to improve their economic stability. This Romanian shipyard, for example, will be brought up to date so that it can compete in the world market.

Union ended the **Cold War** and freed Eastern European countries from oppressive Soviet rule. Like the former Yugoslavian province of Bosnia, many of the countries are politically unstable and economically under-developed. There are often few guarantees of basic human rights.

In 2004, ten former Soviet republics become members of the EU. For more than ten years, the EU helped get them ready for membership. Billions of EU dollars were invested in building new factories and trans-portation systems. Programs were set up to improve schools and to provide vocational, or job, training. The EU also improved health-care systems and other social services. The EU has invested over $11 billion on government reform projects alone in Eastern Europe since 1991 to promote democracy in these countries.

The EU also has become the major trading partner for Russia. Today, it accounts for almost half of Russia's global trade. There are even talks underway of including Russia in a free trade pact someday.

What about the Swiss?

Switzerland, a small country about half the size of the state of Maine, is one of the richest nations in Europe. It is right in the middle of the EU, one of the world's largest trading zones. Yet the Swiss have chosen not to strengthen their trading positions by joining. Why not? For one thing, Swiss banks attract investors from all over the world. Their financial institutions control more than $800 billion in assets. That makes Switzerland—especially Zurich (above)—the world's third-largest financial center. Even more important, for nearly five hundred years, the Swiss have prided themselves on being a **neutral** country. They even stayed neutral during both world wars. They feel that they would lose their neutrality if they became a member of a trading group with political dealings all over the world. The Swiss have entered into some smaller trade agreements, but only when they felt it would not jeopardize their neutrality.

The World Trade Organization

In 1995, the EU helped create the World Trade Organization (WTO). The WTO is the only international organization that sets global rules of trade among nations. Its main function is to ensure that trade flows as smoothly, fairly, and freely as possible. By 2003, the WTO had 145 member countries. Not everyone supports the principles of the trade group. Many people all over the world protest its policies. They think that it favors larger, more developed countries and that it puts trade concerns above health and environmental concerns. Some say it actually hurts the economies of developing nations.

Euro-Arab Dialogues

The EU has a great commitment to peace in the Middle East. From 1994 to 1998, the EU provided $2.3 billion in aid and technical assistance to the Palestinian Authority and the United Nations Relief and Works Agency. However, many people in Arab countries are concerned that the issue of illegal immigrants is causing increasing mistrust and resentment between Europe and the Arab world. A large percentage of illegal immigrants into EU countries come from the Middle East, where they face overpopulation and joblessness.

Moroccan university student Nashiema Chafik wants to see more of the "Euro-Arab Dialogue" projects that the EU has been sponsoring. In 2002, she attended one in Rabat, Morocco. Europeans and Arabs from Egypt, Morocco, Tunisia, Palestine, Holland, Belgium, France, Italy, and Spain met to discuss such issues as social welfare, human rights, and democracy. They talked about unemployment and health care. What Nashiema found most interesting were ideas that would help bring good jobs into her

Around the world, some people protest the work of the World Trade Organization, saying that it does more harm than good. Here, garlic farmers in South Korea were protesting trade agreements that allow foreign-grown garlic to be imported.

country. Nashiema learned how Morocco could get more foreign businesses to invest in it. She heard ideas about increasing trade and developing better agricultural programs. Like others who participated in the dialogue, Nashiema hoped the talks about religious and cultural diversity would help promote peace between Arabs and Europeans.

Economic Aid from the EU

The EU is now by far the largest donor of economic aid to other nations, surpassing the United States. A cornerstone of its aid policy is allowing developing nations to export manufactured goods to the EU duty-free, which provides a huge market that will help them develop. The EU also provides a great deal of money for economic and social development.

Fanuel Singizi, owner of a sugar refinery in Bulawayo, Zimbabwe, appreciates EU aid. His country is one of the seventy-seven African, Caribbean, and Pacific nations that benefit from the Cotonou Agreement of June 2000. Under the agreement, the EU promises economic aid and investment to a country for a period of twenty years. It promises to build up industries, improve transportation, and set up health and social service agencies. In return, the governments of the aided

In one project in Burkino Faso, funds available under the Cotonou Agreement help these women develop a business in sun-dried fruits.

As part of the Cotonou Agreement, the EU supports the training of forest managers to develop the sustainable growth of tropical forests, such as this one in Papua New Guinea.

countries have to promise to work for democracy and the protection of human rights. The EU budgeted $12.4 billion for the first five years of the Cotonou Agreement alone.

In 2001, EU funds helped Fanuel Singizi expand his refinery. He now employs 120 workers and exports twice as much sugar to Europe as he used to. His most fervent hope, however, is that the agreement will help stop the violence and human-rights abuses that have plagued his country for the past few years.

The EU has very specific conditions to continuing their economic aid. The Zimbabwean government must stop harassing its political opponents. It must stop the illegal occupation of farms owned by white farmers. The EU wants guarantees of free elections, freedom of the press, and a fair judicial system. It wants an end to violence. Zimbabweans like Fanuel Singizi hope that promises of continued EU aid will bring about these changes.

Chapter Five

Co-Leaders of the World

Headlines in European newspapers on March 21, 2001, called U.S. President George W. Bush's announcement an "outrage," a "scandal," and a "disaster." The French environment minister called Bush's attitude "entirely provocative and irresponsible." The British environment minister said Bush was ignoring "the most dangerous and fearful challenge to humanity over the next one hundred years."

What had them so angry was the president's attitude toward global warming. Most scientists now believe that the so-called **greenhouse gases** created by automobile and industrial pollution are gradually raising the average temperature of the world. A six-degree change could cause a tremendous increase in droughts, tornadoes, floods, and other extreme weather conditions. Major parts of the world would become totally uninhabitable. The United States produces more than 25 percent of the world's greenhouse gas emissions. The issue has taken a back-seat in the news since the September 11, 2001, terrorist attacks on New York and Washington, D.C., but it is still a hot—and very sore—subject for many people.

In 1997, 154 nations met in Japan to draft an agree-ment called the Kyoto **Protocol**. This pact, when it is finally **ratified**, will

Demonstrators in Sweden carried a giant head of U.S. President George Bush through the streets to protest his 2001 rejection of the Kyoto Protocol.

U$A THE ENEMY OF HUMANITY

require industrialized nations to substantially reduce the emission of greenhouse gases by the year 2012. When it came time to sign the pact, President Bush reversed the initial United States commitment, made under President Clinton, and refused to sign it. He said, "I will not accept anything that will harm our economy and hurt our workers. We have an energy shortage."

The EU is taking many different approaches to improving the environment. These electricity-generating windmills are in Scotland.

Three months later, President Bush made his first presidential visit to Europe. Everywhere he went, he got a personal taste of Europe's criticism about Kyoto. In Göteborg, Sweden, rowdy demonstrators carried a huge, ugly, papier-mâché likeness of Bush's head through the streets. Some marched right up to the president's hotel and dropped their trousers to express their displeasure. More than two hundred people were arrested for throwing rocks and bottles. According to the European press, people were angry not just about the U.S. policies. They were upset about Bush's "aggressive and arrogant manner" in expressing them.

The EU has since accused the Bush administration of initiating new government policies within the United States that could actually increase U.S. greenhouse-gas emissions by up to 30 percent instead of cutting them. The EU continues to put pressure on Bush to sign the Kyoto pact. President Bush has stated that while he doesn't agree with the agreement, "We do agree that climate change is a serious issue, and we must work together." Bush has also received criticism at home from many Americans for rejecting the Kyoto Protocol.

EU and U.S.: World Leaders at Odds

The Kyoto controversy reflects how the EU's role in world politics has grown and changed. It is also an example of how the EU and United States do not always agree in matters of world leadership.

On May 31, 2002, all fifteen member states of the EU ratified the Kyoto Protocol without the U.S. signature. United Nations Secretary-General Kofi Annan welcomed the move, saying it was "good news for the entire world." Among the other major nations still expected to ratify the agreement are Russia, Japan, and China. The number of ratifying nations will then exceed the fifty-five needed to make the treaty legal.

ECHO is the European Commission's Humanitarian Aid Office, one of the primary donors of humanitarian food in the world. Here, Emma Bonino, a European Commissioner, meets with women in Afghanistan for ECHO.

There was a time when such a treaty would have fallen apart if superpower United States backed out of it. Many of Kyoto's supporters were afraid that was exactly what was going to happen. But the EU used its new political clout to help keep the treaty on track. It is also pressuring the United States to sign it, pointing out that the world's biggest polluter should do its part.

Partners for a Strong World Economy

While the United States and the EU disagree on some issues, they continue to be partners on many issues. A large part of their cooperation is based on shared values. Both have a strong respect for democracy, the rule of law, an open market economy, and fundamental human rights. The European Union and the United States together account for more than 30 percent of world trade. Together, they have worked hard to increase global trade. They also have a large number of businesses that invest directly in each other's economies. These billions of dollars in investments create many jobs on both sides of the Atlantic.

The United States and the EU also work together to create economic development programs throughout the world. Some of those EU-U.S. actions support rebuilding efforts and **humanitarian** aid for people in the former Yugoslavia and Afghanistan. Their joint actions also contribute to the Middle East peace process. The EU and United States have also cooperated to address global challenges such as migration, the AIDS crisis, the environment, international crime, and the war on terrorism.

Partners with Strong Disagreements

The EU and the United States are in fundamental agreement on most trade, peacekeeping, and humanitarian issues, but some issues cause conflicts. For example, many representatives in the EU government believe that foods with chemical or hormone additives are dangerous. They look closely at imported products to see what effect they could have on the environment and question whether enough research has been done on new drugs imported into the EU. International companies such as Coca-Cola and Microsoft have to conform to very strict EU laws about how they manufacture, advertise, and sell their products. Even if the companies don't violate U.S. laws, they can be prosecuted in EU courts. The companies then appeal to the U.S. government for support.

There are larger areas of disagreement, such as how to establish peace

Enhanced Beef —
Tastier or More Dangerous?

Injecting cattle with hormones to make the animals grow larger is a common practice in the United States. The EU bans the importing of beef produced from cattle treated with hormones because it believes the hormones may be dangerous to people eating the beef. In response to the EU's ban on U.S. beef imports, the United States imposed huge tariffs on food it imports from Europe. This includes French exports such as wine, paté, chocolates, and Roquefort cheese. In 2002, the outraged French Agriculture Minister Jean Glavany called American food "the worst food in the world." He said it was dangerous and unsafe. His statement made U.S. Agriculture Secretary Dan Glickman angry. The United States promptly imposed tariffs on $191 million of EU handbags, bed linens, and other luxury goods. Two French farmers' unions started a campaign urging European consumers to boycott American goods.

Efforts are being made on both sides to reach an agreement on the use of growth hormones in beef to be imported into the European Union.

in the Middle East and how best to fight global terrorism. The EU is divided on when and how to create a separate Palestinian state alongside Israel. Some member countries, such as Britain, agreed with the United States that the leader of Iraq had weapons of mass destruction available to terrorists and should be ousted from power, by force if necessary. Most EU members did not believe there was a direct connection between Iraq and terrorism and wanted to resolve the issue of the possibility of Iraq's possessing such weapons by more peaceful methods.

When the United States decided to take military action against Iraq in March of 2003, EU member Britain sided with the United States on its right to invade Iraq and replace its leader Saddam Hussein. Other EU nations, however, such as France and Germany, were strongly opposed to using such force. They believed that any military action should be approved by the United Nations first.

The United States also disagrees with most EU member nations regarding membership in the EU for Turkey. The United States administration believes that Turkey is ready for EU membership, despite Turkey's human-rights abuses and its reluctance to solve the problem of Cyprus.

In early 2003, when the EU opposed the U.S. stand on the invasion of Iraq, British prime minister Tony Blair (left) was able to quietly discuss the possible war with French prime minister Jacques Chirac (right) at an EU meeting.

The EU and the Future

The European Union is a continually evolving and changing creation. When members met to sign the Maastricht Treaty in 1993, they agreed to meet again in Nice, France, in 2000 to discuss further growth and changes. The Treaty of Nice of 2000 included a Declaration on the Future of the Union. In it, the EU called for a more in-depth discussion and debate about the future of Europe and about improving the structure of the European Union. The changes allowed the European Union to be enlarged. It may eventually have twenty-seven states.

No one doubts that the development of the European Union during

43

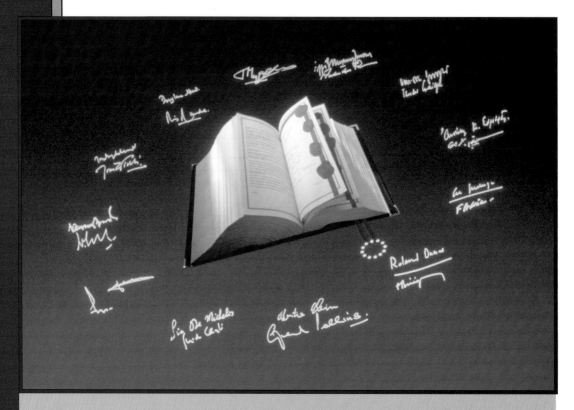

The Maastricht Treaty (shown here with the signatures of representatives of the countries that signed it in 1993) created a European Union and prepared it to develop into a larger organization that is able and willing to be one of the leaders of the world.

the second half of the twentieth century changed Europe for coming centuries. Through its search for "ever closer union," the European Union has helped bring both economic and political stability to the European nations since the fall of communism in 1991. It has become an international trading partner equal to the United States. The EU's roles as mediator, peacekeeper, and provider of humanitarian aid are sure to grow in the coming years as it becomes an even more significant player on the world stage.

Time Line

1951 Belgium, France, the Federal Republic of Germany, Italy, Luxembourg, and the Netherlands sign the Treaty of Paris to create the European Coal and Steel Community (ECSC).

1958 The Treaties of Rome go into effect, setting up the European Economic Community (EEC or Common Market) and the European Atomic Energy Community (EURATOM).

1967 The ECSC, EEC, and EURATOM merge to become the European Community (EC).

1973 The United Kingdom, Ireland, and Denmark join the European Community.

1981 Greece becomes the tenth member state of the EC.

1986 Spain and Portugal become the eleventh and twelfth member states of the EC.

1990 East and West Germany are reunited after the fall of the Berlin Wall.

1991 The Soviet Union collapses; many of its republics become independent nations eventually eligible for membership in the EU.

1993 Maastricht Treaty (Treaty on European Union) is ratified, creating single-market European Union (EU).

1994 The EU and the seven-member European Free Trade Association (EFTA) (non-EU members) form the European Economic Area.

1995 Austria, Finland, and Sweden join the European Union.

1999 The euro is introduced in twelve participating member states; the Treaty of Amsterdam institutes government reforms, emphasizing citizenship and individual rights.

2000 The Treaty of Nice continues the reform process and invites ten new countries for 2004 membership.

2002 The euro currency is fully launched.

2004 Poland, Hungary, the Czech Republic, Slovakia, Slovenia, Estonia, Lithuania, Latvia, Malta, and Cyprus are scheduled to become members.

Glossary

additive a substance added to another one in relatively small amounts to cause a change in properties

appeal a legal action in which an earlier court decision is brought to a higher court with the goal of reversing or changing that decision

cabinet minister usually a department head in a government; one of the president's or prime minister's advisors

Cold War the period of political tension between Communist and non-Communist countries from the end of World War II until the collapse of the Soviet Union in 1990

diplomacy the art of conducting negotiations among governments

greenhouse gases the gases that are generated by automotive engines and coal-burning industries and accumulate in the atmosphere, forming a heat-holding blanket around Earth

hormone a chemical produced by a living body or by scientists that produces an effect on other cells

human rights rights that people are born with, such as freedom and dignity

humanitarian promoting human welfare and social reform

nationalistic characterized by loyalty and devotion to a nation

Nazi belonging to the National Socialist party under Adolf Hitler in Germany from 1933 to 1945

neutral not in favor of one side or the other; in the middle

protocol agreement or draft of an agreement

ratify to give formal approval

refugee a person who is forced to flee his home, either to a different place in his own country or to another country, usually because of war

tariff a tax imposed by a government on imports or exports

To Find Out More

BOOKS

Petersen, David. *Europe*. True Book Series. Children's Press, 1998.
Powell, Jillian. *European Union*. World Organizations Series.
    Franklin Watts, 2001.

ADDRESSES AND WEB SITES

European Commission
Rue de la Loi 200
B – 1049 Brussels
Belgium

Delegation of the European Commission to the United States
2300 M Street, NW
Washington, DC 20037
www.eurunion.org

The European Union for Young People
www.eurunion.org/infores/teaching/Young/EUYoungPeople.htm

The EU Observer
www.euobserver.com/index.phtml?sid=18

Europa: The European Union On-Line
europa.eu.int/

Index